The Life and World of
MONTEZUMA

KT-115-959

Struan Reid

Heinemann
LIBRARY

H www.heinemann.co.uk/library
Visit our website to find out more information about Heinemann Library books.

To order:
☎ Phone 44 (0) 1865 888066
📄 Send a fax to 44 (0) 1865 314091
💻 Visit the Heinemann Library Bookshop at www.heinemann.co.uk/library to browse our catalogue and order online.

First published in Great Britain by Heinemann Library,
Halley Court, Jordan Hill, Oxford OX2 8EJ
a division of Reed Educational and Professional Publishing Ltd.
Heinemann is a registered trademark of Reed Educational & Professional Publishing Ltd.

OXFORD MELBOURNE AUCKLAND
JOHANNESBURG BLANTYRE GABORONE
IBADAN PORTSMOUTH (NH) USA CHICAGO

© Reed Educational and Professional Publishing Ltd 2002
The moral right of the proprietor has been asserted.

All rights reserved. No part of this publication may be reproduced, stored in a retrieval system, or transmitted in any form or by any means, electronic, mechanical, photocopying, recording, or otherwise without either the prior written permission of the Publishers or a licence permitting restricted copying in the United Kingdom issued by the Copyright Licensing Agency Ltd, 90 Tottenham Court Road, London W1P 0LP.

Designed by Celia Floyd
Illustrated by Jeff Edwards and Joanna Brooker
Originated by Ambassador Litho Ltd
Printed by Wing King Tong in Hong Kong

ISBN 0 431 14763 9
06 05 04 03 02
10 9 8 7 6 5 4 3 2 1

British Library Cataloguing in Publication Data

Reid, Struan
  The life and world of Montezuma
  1. Montezuma, II, Emperor of Mexico, ca. 1480–1520
  2. Emperors – Mexico – Biography – Juvenile literature
  3. Mexico – History – To 1519 – Juvenile literature
  I. Title II. Montezuma
  972'.018'092

Acknowledgements

The Publishers would like to thank the following for permission to reproduce photographs: AKG: p12; The Art Archive: pp7, 10, 13, 15, 16, 17, 18, 19, 20, 21, 22, 23, 24, 26, 27; Bridgeman: pp5, 6, 9, 14, 29; Corbis: pp8, 11, 25; South America Pictures: p28.

Cover photograph reproduced with permission of The Art Archive.

Our thanks to Rebecca Vickers for her help in the preparation of this book.

Every effort has been made to contact copyright holders of any material reproduced in this book. Any omissions will be rectified in subsequent printings if notice is given to the Publisher.

Education

Library Service

LEARNING RESOURCES FOR SCHOOLS

0 8 JUL 2003

CLASS NO.

972

Contents

Any words appearing in the text in bold, **like this**, are explained in the glossary.

Who was Montezuma?

Montezuma was a great king and warrior who lived 500 years ago. He ruled over the huge, rich and powerful Aztec **Empire** in the land now known as Mexico. His territory stretched from the Atlantic to the Pacific Ocean and contained more than 500 towns. The capital city was called Tenochtitlán and it was one of the largest and most beautiful cities in the world.

Strangers arrive

In the year 1519, Montezuma received disturbing news. Strange-looking men had arrived in his lands and were marching towards Tenochtitlán. What made him nervous was that these reports seemed to confirm ancient **prophecies** that the Aztec Empire would one day be destroyed by angry and **vengeful** gods.

In fact, the strangers were not gods at all, but soldiers who had sailed across the Atlantic Ocean from Spain. They had come to conquer the Aztec Empire. Only 25 years earlier, Europeans had had no idea that the continents of North and South America even existed. Then, in 1492, an Italian explorer, called Christopher Columbus, sailed westward from Spain and arrived in this 'New World'.

The Aztec Empire

The Aztecs lived in the area of land joining North and South America, now Mexico. Over 3000 years, this region saw the rise of many great civilizations, including the Olmecs, Zapotecs, Maya and Toltecs. The last of these was the Aztecs. They conquered and ruled a huge empire from about 1420 until 1520.

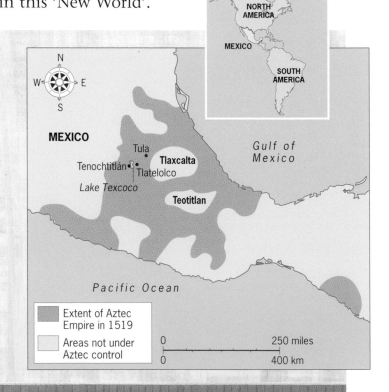

NORTH AMERICA

MEXICO

SOUTH AMERICA

N
W — E
S

MEXICO

Tula

Tlaxcalta

Tenochtitlán

Tlatelolco

Lake Texcoco

Teotitlan

Gulf of Mexico

Pacific Ocean

Extent of Aztec Empire in 1519

Areas not under Aztec control

0   250 miles
0   400 km

The end of the empire

The Aztecs fought to try and stop the Spaniards from conquering their lands, but within two years Montezuma was dead. His empire had been destroyed and most of the Aztec **civilization** was in ruins. The prophecies had come true, and Montezuma had been the last great ruler of this brilliant empire.

▲ This headdress, which may have belonged to Montezuma, was made from the tail feathers of the quetzal bird. Only high-ranking Aztec **officials** and warriors were allowed to wear feathered garments.

Key dates

1325	City of Tenochtitlán founded
1420	Growth of Aztec Empire begins
1492	Christopher Columbus sails to the Americas
1502	Montezuma becomes emperor
1517	First Spanish expedition reaches Mexico
1520	Death of Montezuma
1521	Tenochtitlán falls to Spanish invaders
1535	Aztec Empire now under Spanish rule; known as New Spain

Montezuma's early life

Montezuma was born in about 1466. His parents were members of the Aztec royal family. A relation of his father, who was also called Montezuma, was **emperor** when baby Montezuma was born. The young boy was brought up as a royal prince.

Montezuma's arrival in the world would have been greeted with celebrations. As soon as Montezuma was born, an **astrologer** would have been sent to the royal palace to help the family choose a name for the prince, which was a very important decision. Using a calendar of stars, the astrologer also calculated the lucky day on which to name the baby.

▼ **Emperor Montezuma is seated on a throne on the left. He is receiving goods such as jaguar skins, woven cloaks and shields from the cities of his empire. This illustration is from a 16th-century Spanish account of the Aztecs.**

▲ Aztec writing did not use letters and words, instead they used pictures called glyphs. The dots are numbers. These pictures show the names of four of the days of the month: 5 wind, 6 house, 7 lizard and 8 snake.

Montezuma's family

Like all Aztec noblemen, Montezuma's father had a number of wives, so Montezuma was brought up with many half-brothers and sisters. The family lived in rooms on the top floor of the huge, sprawling royal palace that lay at the heart of Tenochtitlán. Montezuma and his brothers and sisters had endless rooms and corridors to explore and beautiful gardens to play in.

School days

Montezuma was sent to school at an early age. The school was called a *calmecac* and there he was taught with the sons of other noble families. Discipline was very strict and the pupils were punished if they put a foot wrong. The boys learned reading and writing, astrology, **law**, and mathematics. Their lessons trained them to become priests, **judges** and army officers. Because he was a member of the royal family, Montezuma was educated as a possible ruler of the Aztec **Empire**.

Religious training

Religion was extremely important to all Aztecs. Montezuma and his classmates were given a very strict religious training. They were taught to pray and to **fast**. Aztec religion could be very bloodthirsty. The boys also had to perform special **rituals** in which they cut and pierced their own flesh.

Warfare and games

All Aztec men, from the **emperor** down, were brought up to fight in battle. As he was growing up, Montezuma was taught the skills of warfare. He took part in mock fights with other boys, using wooden swords and shields. By the time he reached the age of eighteen, Montezuma had already fought in a number of real battles.

A brave warrior

No Aztec, not even a royal prince, could be honoured as a true **nobleman** until he had captured live prisoners in battle. Once he had done this, Montezuma was recognized as a brave and experienced warrior. As a young boy he had worn his hair long and uncut. Now, as a grown man and a warrior, he was allowed to wear it shorter and tied up in a small bunch, called a topknot, on top of his head.

▶ An Aztec soldier who had taken four prisoners in battle could join the special eagle or jaguar troops. This figure is an eagle warrior, wearing armour shaped like an eagle's head and wings.

Playing games

Life for the young Montezuma was not all strict lessons and fighting. He and his schoolmates also enjoyed playing games, such as the ball game called *tlachtli*. Only noblemen could play *tlachtli*, as it was part of their religious upbringing, but everyone came to watch and cheer.

Two teams tried to get a small, hard rubber ball through a stone ring mounted high up on a wall. The players were not allowed to touch the ball with their hands – it could only be hit with their hips, elbows or knees. *Tlachtli* could be dangerous because the ball moved at great speed. Players were often injured and sometimes even killed.

Music and dance

Montezuma was taught to play musical instruments and also learned how to perform special dances for religious ceremonies. Music, song and dance were enjoyed by everyone and, like almost everything in Aztec life, were closely linked to religion.

▲ This picture shows a group of Aztec musicians. The two men in the middle are playing drums, and the others are playing rattles made from **gourds**.

Aztec society

The Aztecs had not always lived in Mexico. According to their own **legends**, they moved there from a land to the north, which they called Aztlan. For many years the Aztecs wandered through deserts. Then, in about 1325, they settled on an island in the middle of a lake called Texcoco. There they began to build houses and temples. They called the site Tenochtitlán, which means 'Place of the Fruit of the Cactus'. This marked the beginning of the Aztecs' rise to power.

▲ According to legend, the god Huitzilopochtli ordered the Aztecs to settle where they saw an eagle in a cactus, with a serpent in its beak. They spotted this strange sight on an island in Lake Texcoco, where they **founded** Tenochtitlán.

From emperor down to slave

As **emperor**, Montezuma was the most important person in Aztec society. Below Montezuma were the great nobles called *pipiltrin*, who owned land and *tecuhtli* who helped him to rule. They were the generals and **judges** who ran the daily life in the cities. Most Aztec people were the *maceualtin*, or common people. The lowest group of all were the slaves. Some were prisoners of war. Others were Aztecs who had fallen on hard times.

The Aztec gods

The Aztecs worshipped many different gods. As well as being the ruler of his people, Montezuma was also the Aztec high priest, the most important religious leader. It was important that the gods were kept happy and the best way of doing this, the Aztecs believed, was to give them human blood. Aztec priests **sacrificed** thousands of men, women and children to the war and sun god, Huitzilopochtli. He was given a daily diet of human hearts to make sure that he would rise the next morning. When Montezuma became emperor, he would have had to perform some of these sacrifices.

▶ This skull is decorated with turquoise mosaic. It represents Tezcatlipoca, the Aztec god of fate.

Two Calendars

The Aztecs had two calendars. The first was called *xiuhpohualli*, 'the counting of the years'. It was used to work out the seasons. This was very important for planning the farming year. The second calendar, called the *tonalpohualli*, 'the counting of the days', was used by priests and astrologers to predict the future.

Montezuma the emperor

At the age of about twenty, Montezuma would have married. He was allowed to marry a number of wives. He was elected **emperor** in 1502, at the age of about 36. The new emperor was not always the son of the previous emperor, and Montezuma succeeded his great-uncle, Ahuitzotl. Montezuma was chosen from all the royal princes by a council of nobles, priests and military leaders, because they believed that he had the best qualities to be emperor.

Montezuma's coronation

After his election, Montezuma had to spend four days alone in the temple of the sun god, Huitzilopochtli. There he **fasted** and **meditated** in preparation for the difficult work he had been chosen to do. At Montezuma's **coronation** ceremony, many religious **sacrifices** were made in the temples, followed by a great feast in the royal palace. The leaders of the peoples ruled by the Aztecs were ordered to attend the coronation to show their respect for the new emperor.

◀ All Aztec soldiers carried a shield for protection, but only high-ranking warriors were allowed to have feathered shields. This one was given to Cortés by Montezuma. It is decorated with a picture of a coyote, the name symbol of Emperor Ahuitzolt.

Treated like a god

Montezuma usually only appeared in public at religious ceremonies. When he did, his nobles carried him in a special golden chair, called a litter. He wore splendid clothes, gold jewellery and a feather headdress. No one was allowed to look him directly in the face, so people near him had to bow down and keep their eyes looking at the ground. When Montezuma stepped down from his litter, the floor where he walked was swept and the nobles took off their cloaks and spread them out before him so that his feet never touched the ground.

▲ The Aztecs made jewellery from gold and precious stones such as turquoise and jade. This turquoise ornament, in the shape of a snake, would have been worn on the chest of a priest.

Warlord

Montezuma was chosen to be emperor because of his bravery in battle. After his coronation, he had to prove that he was a good leader by capturing live prisoners to be sacrificed to the gods. Montezuma was away fighting for most of the first fifteen years of his reign.

Family life

When Montezuma was in Tenochtitlán, he lived in the royal palace at the heart of the city. The palace was so huge that one Spanish visitor later wrote: 'I walked until I was tired, and never saw the whole of it.' It was a magnificent building, containing hundreds of rooms on two floors. Outside, the palace was surrounded by gardens with ponds and fountains, and even a large zoo where Montezuma kept wild and exotic animals and birds.

At home with the family

Montezuma and his wives and children lived on the top floor of the palace. There were separate women's quarters, where his wives and daughters spent much of their time spinning, weaving and making beautiful embroideries. Montezuma always looked very splendid when he appeared in public. At home with his family, however, he lived a very simple life and his private rooms were plainly decorated.

◄ One of Montezuma's attendants dresses the **emperor** in a **ceremonial** robe and headdress for a public appearance.

Inic .v. parrapho ipan mioa imзquitla
mantli minechichioaya mtlatoque ioã
incioapipiltin.

▲ All Aztec men wore a **loincloth** and a cloak. This person is a **nobleman** and his clothes are embroidered and decorated with feathers to show his wealth. The woman wears a loose, decorated blouse over an embroidered skirt.

A room for every occasion

The palace was not just Montezuma's home. He also used it to entertain his nobles, to see his advisers and to meet **governors** from the different parts of his **empire**. As many as 600 people would visit him at the palace every day, and there were special guest rooms where visiting **ambassadors** could stay. Most of the rooms on the ground floor were used for special occasions, and one of them was so big that it could seat 3000 people. Many of the walls of these official rooms were covered with beautiful paintings, stone and wood carvings and panels of solid gold.

Palace staff

With so many people visiting every day, thousands of servants were needed to run the palace. There were special rooms for builders and cleaners, for Montezuma's bodyguards and for the royal servants and slaves. There were huge kitchens where the food for the royal feasts was cooked, and storerooms where all the supplies were kept.

Montezuma's empire

Montezuma ruled his **empire** with the help of his **noblemen**, army leaders, **judges** and city leaders. Many of the important positions in the government of the empire were held by his relatives. The most important person after Montezuma was his chief adviser. This person, although always a man, was known as the *Cihuacoatl*, which means 'snake woman'. He was the chief judge and was in charge of thousands of government **officials**. He also supervised the election of a new **emperor**.

One of the biggest cities in the world

Montezuma's capital city of Tenochtitlán had a population of at least 80,000 people, perhaps even as many as 300,000. This was more than many European cities at that time. It was a beautiful city, full of stone and wooden buildings, clean wide streets and many **canals**. In the fields outside the city, the people grew crops of maize and peppers, and cotton for making cloth.

▼ This plan of Montezuma's capital city, Tenochtitlán, was drawn by the Spaniards. It shows the city on an island in the lake, and the causeways that linked it to the mainland.

Paying tribute

There were so many people living in the city that they could not possibly grow all the things they needed themselves. The Aztecs had to rely on extra supplies from other parts of their empire.

Every few months, lists of the things needed by the people of Tenochtitlán were sent out to the other **city-states** in the empire. Goods such as **grain**, fruit and vegetables, cloth, weapons and feather headdresses were collected and delivered to Tenochtitlán, where they were stored in huge warehouses. This is called **tribute**. These demands for tribute made the Aztecs very unpopular with the people.

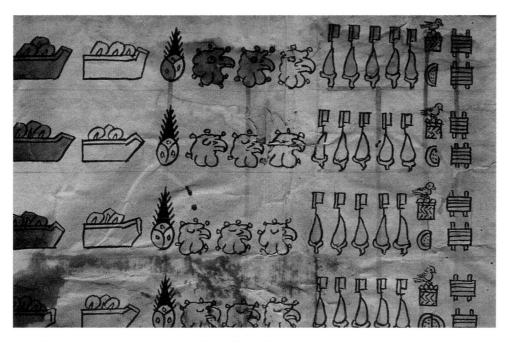

▲ The Aztecs used tribute lists like this one to show what goods a town had to pay. The symbols above the goods show how many were needed: the tree symbol means 400 and the flag 20.

Picking fights

The other cities in the empire could refuse to pay tribute, but if they dared to do this they would be attacked by the Aztecs. The Aztecs were almost always fighting with their neighbours. These wars supplied the Aztecs with the great number of prisoners they needed for their human **sacrifices** to the gods.

Warnings from the gods

To the Aztec people, Montezuma seemed to be the most powerful ruler in the world. He was a brave warrior and a brilliant war-leader. Riches poured into Tenochtitlán from every part of the **empire**. Montezuma was treated as if he were a god. In 1518 he was at the peak of his power, but that year the lives of the Aztecs would change for ever.

Strange omens

Strange things had been happening that disturbed the great **emperor**. For several years now Montezuma and his advisers had received **omens** that something terrible was going to take place. A **comet** was seen blazing in a streak of flames across the skies. Temples were struck by bolts of lightening and burst into flames and Tenochtitlán was hit by sudden floods. Some said they had seen the water in Lake Texcoco boil, others said that in the middle of the night they had heard the voice of a woman, telling them to run away from the city.

The legend of Quetzalcóatl

At this time, Montezuma was probably reminded of the legend of the god Quetzalcóatl. Long ago, he had been driven out of the Aztec lands and had sailed away eastward across the seas. One day, it was said, he would come back to destroy the Aztec Empire and take the land for himself.

▶ Quetzalcóatl, the Aztec god of creation, could take many forms. He was often shown as a snake with a green feathered tail. This turquoise mask shows him in his human shape.

▲ This picture shows Montezuma standing on the roof of his palace, watching a comet in the sky. Aztec **astrologers** took this comet as a sign of bad things to come.

A look into the future?

One of the strangest of all these stories concerned some fishermen, who were said to have caught an extraordinary grey bird on the shores of Lake Texcoco. It had a mirror on its head and looked so odd that the fishermen brought it to show to the emperor. When Montezuma looked into the mirror, he saw warriors, riding on strange-looking beasts, who had come to destroy his empire.

Strangers on
the coast

One day, towards the end of 1519, messengers arrived in Tenochtitlán, bringing Montezuma worrying news. They reported that a small army of strange-looking men had been seen on the coast. These men had pale skins and beards. They had arrived in huge craft, as big as mountains, and were riding on four-legged monsters. Montezuma had spies working for him all over the **empire**. They watched the strangers closely and every day sent back reports to their master. Montezuma learned that the strangers were dressed from head to toe in metal skins and carried terrifying weapons that spat fire.

▲ This picture shows the arrival of the first Spanish ship on the coast of Mexico. An Aztec is hiding in the tree, watching and waiting to report what he has seen.

Men or gods?

Montezuma was probably in a panic. These reports would have confirmed his greatest fear – the god Quetzalcóatl had returned at last to reclaim his kingdom. How was Montezuma supposed to deal with these unwelcome visitors? If they really were gods, then they would have to be welcomed and treated with respect. But supposing that they were not gods? If they were soldiers who had come to attack his empire, he would have to fight them.

Adventurers from Spain

In fact, the visitors were a band of about 500 Spanish soldiers. The 'craft as big as mountains' that they travelled in were ships, and the 'four-legged monsters' they rode were horses. They were led by a soldier and **adventurer**, called Hernán Cortés, and had come in search of a land full of gold and treasure.

By an amazing coincidence, the very day that Cortés and his men arrived in Mexico was also the birthday of Quetzalcóatl. This was exactly the time when Aztec legends claimed that the god would return to destroy their empire.

▶ Hernán Cortés, leader of the Spanish soldiers. He is wearing armour, which the Aztecs thought was a metal skin.

Hernán Cortés (1485–1547)

Hernán Cortés had read stories of the great riches to be found in the Americas, and came to Mexico in search of gold. In 1519 he set out to capture the Aztec Empire and claim it for Spain. From 1524–26 Cortés ruled as **governor** of 'New Spain', as the empire became known, but he eventually fell from power and died forgotten in southern Spain.

Montezuma panics

As Montezuma heard more about the visitors to his lands he probably grew very frightened. His spies sent him reports every day, and he learned that the strangers had even asked questions about him and wanted to meet him. But at first Montezuma did nothing. He sat alone in his palace and waited.

Gifts of gold

Then Montezuma decided to send gifts to the strangers. One of the gifts was a huge dish made of solid gold. This present may have been intended as a warning to the visitors that Montezuma was the richest and most powerful ruler in the world, so that they had better leave. However, these rich gifts did not warn off the Spaniards, but only made them want more gold.

Montezuma probably hoped that these unwelcome visitors would just go away. But when the Spaniards had arrived in Mexico, they had destroyed their boats, so they could not leave. In August 1519 they started to march towards the heart of Montezuma's **empire**. Along the way, they recruited warriors from enemies of the Aztecs.

▼ Montezuma, seated on his throne, is instructing the messengers he is sending to the Spaniards.

The army arrives

Back in Tenochtitlán, Montezuma heard about the growing army that was heading closer. He sent more messengers to try and persuade them to go away. He set **ambushes** and traps, but nothing could stop them. Finally, the Spaniards and their followers reached the shores of Lake Texcoco and saw the great city of Tenochtitlán for the first time. Montezuma was still unsure whether these strangers were gods or humans. He was about to find out.

▲ This painting shows the princes of Tlaxcalta, a place the Aztecs had not conquered. Here they are agreeing to help the Spaniards fight against the Aztecs.

Doña Marina

One of the people travelling with the Spaniards was a woman called Malintzin, who came from a tribe that hated the Aztecs. The Spaniards named her Doña Marina. She learned to speak Spanish and acted as **interpreter** for Cortés. It was through her help that the Spaniards were able to recruit so many extra warriors.

The death
of Montezuma

The Spaniards began to walk along one of the causeways that led across the lake to Tenochtitlán. Suddenly, coming towards them, they saw a wonderful sight. Montezuma himself had come to greet them. He was being carried in his golden litter and he was dressed in his most splendid **ceremonial** robes. The Spaniards were presented with gifts and Montezuma gave them a speech of welcome.

▲ This picture shows Montezuma and Cortés in the Royal Palace at Tenochtitlán, with Doña Marina as their **interpreter**.

Under arrest

Then they were escorted into the city and housed in one of the smaller royal palaces. The Spaniards were to be the guests of the **emperor**, but Cortés knew that it was only the **goodwill** of Montezuma that prevented them from being killed. He had to act fast. Two weeks after they arrived, Montezuma was suddenly arrested and imprisoned by the Spaniards.

Killed by his own people?

Six months later, fighting broke out between the Aztecs and the Spaniards. The city was in uproar. Cortés ordered Montezuma to speak to his people and calm the situation. but the Aztecs had lost all respect for Montezuma. When he appeared on the palace balcony, the angry crowds threw stones at him. It is said one large stone struck him on the head and Montezuma fell to the floor. He was carried back into the palace, and died soon afterwards.

The Spaniards claimed that Montezuma had died from his head wound, but the Aztecs said that he must have been strangled by the Spaniards. Montezuma had once been treated like a god, but at the end of his life he was hated and despised by his own people.

▶ This gold pendant was made by highly skilled Mixtec craftsmen, who supplied jewellery to the Aztecs.

Hidden treasure

The Spaniards discovered a secret room in the palace where they were staying. When they pulled down the wall, they found that the room was piled high with Montezuma's gold, silver and jewels. This was what they had really sailed all the way from Spain to find.

The end of the Aztec Empire

The Aztecs were now determined to kill the Spaniards who had come to conquer them. Cortés and his men had to leave Tenochtitlán as soon as they could. One night, they tried to escape from the city under the cover of darkness. As they were creeping away, they were attacked by a huge Aztec army that was waiting for them. Many of the Spaniards were killed or dragged away to be **sacrificed** to the gods.

Tenochtitlán under siege

Cortés and some of his men managed to escape. The Aztecs believed that any survivors had run away and would not come back. Cortés had other ideas. He formed a huge new army from the Aztecs' enemies and marched back to Tenochtitlán. They surrounded the city, cutting off the food and water supplies, so the people inside began to starve. For three long months, the Aztecs fought back. Another **emperor**, a nephew of Montezuma's called Cuauhtémoc, had been elected and he swore to his people that he would defend the **empire** to the death.

◄ This picture shows a scene from *La Noche Triste*. As Cortés and his men try to escape, they are attacked by Aztec soldiers, some of them dressed as eagle and jaguar warriors.

La Noche Triste

The night Cortés and his soldiers tried to escape from Tenochtitlán is known as *La Noche Triste*, which means 'the sad night'. More than two-thirds of the Spaniards were killed on the causeway leading across Lake Texcoco. Many of them drowned, weighed down by the gold treasures they had stolen from Montezuma's palace.

The Aztecs surrender

Finally, the Spaniards and their supporters were able to break into the city. There was bitter fighting in the streets, but the Aztecs' weapons were no match for the guns and steel swords of the Spaniards. One day, the new emperor Cuauhtémoc was caught trying to escape from the city. When news of his **treachery** reached the ears of the brave Aztec warriors they surrendered. Tenochtitlán was finally captured by the Spaniards in August 1521. The magnificent city now lay in ruins.

▼ In the battle for Tenochtitlán, Spanish and Aztec soldiers are fighting on one of the causeways. The bodies of dead soldiers are floating in the water nearby.

After Montezuma

When Tenochtitlán fell to the Spaniards, they swept through the ruined city killing thousands of Aztecs. The last Aztec **emperor**, Cuauhtémoc, was at first treated with respect by the Spaniards, but they soon had no further use for him, and one year later they killed him. The remaining Aztec temples were pulled down and the people were forbidden to practise their old religion.

Slavery and disease

Hernán Cortés was appointed **governor** of New Spain, as Montezuma's old **empire** was now called. Christian churches were built on the ruins of many Aztec temples. Thousands of Aztecs and the other peoples who lived in Mexico died from warfare and slavery. Many more were killed by smallpox and other **diseases** that the Spaniards had carried with them from Europe. The Aztecs had no resistance to these diseases. Just 80 years after the death of Montezuma, three-quarters of his people had died out. It was to be 300 years before Mexico won back its **independence** from Spain.

▼ The Spaniards built a huge cathedral on the site of the Great Temple that stood next to Montezuma's palace. These ruins are all that is left of the Great Temple today.

Legacy of the Aztecs

The people of Mexico today have inherited many Aztec and Spanish traditions. The descendants of the Aztecs are now known as the Nahua. The Aztec language is still spoken in parts of Mexico and some of the old Aztec religious ceremonies are still celebrated there as part of the Christian religion. Montezuma's family lived on for many generations. His eldest son was created 'Count of Montezuma' by the King of Spain and some of his descendants eventually became **governors** of New Spain.

How do we know?

We know about Montezuma and the Aztecs from the **records** they kept and from the accounts written by their Spanish conquerors. The Aztecs recorded their history and details of their daily lives, laws, gods and **customs** in books now called codices. Many of these were destroyed by the Spaniards, but a few survived.

▲ Montezuma, emperor of the Aztecs, being carried in his golden litter. The Spanish artist, Miguel Gonzalez, has shown Montezuma wearing a European-style crown and clothes.

Most of the Aztec buildings and the objects inside them were also destroyed. The few objects that survived, such as pottery, embroidery and sculptures, provide us with valuable information about the Aztecs.

Glossary

adventurer person who looks for adventure, and especially who looks for success or money through daring deeds

ambassadors representatives sent by the government of a ruling group or country to visit other rulers or countries

ambush sudden attack from a hidden position

astrology study of the stars and planets. An astrologer is someone who tries to predict the future from the stars.

canal artifical waterway built to water crops or for transport

ceremonial something that forms part of a formal ceremony

city-state separate state limited to the area within the city walls and the land nearby

civilization large group of people who live in an organized society with laws and a system of religion

comet huge ball of dust, ice and gas that travels around the Sun, often followed by a tail of gas

coronation ceremony for crowning a monarch

custom a practice or habit, or the usual way of doing something

disease illness

emperor ruler of an empire

empire large area of land ruled by a single person

fast stop eating all or certain foods, especially for religious reasons

found start something, such as a city or school

goodwill friendly feelings

gourd hard-skinned fruit of a trailing plant in the pumpkin family. The hollowed skin can be used as a container.

governor someone who rules a city or land for another person, such as a king

grain seeds from grasses that can be eaten, such as corn

independence state of being free from the control of others

interpreter person who translates from one language to another

judge official who presides over a court of law and passes judgement

law rule or set of rules set by a court to control people's behaviour

legend ancient story

loincloth a piece of cloth worn hanging down, front and back from the waist

meditate think deeply about something, especially a religious or spiritual matter

nobleman man of the highest rank in Aztec society after the emperor

official person who holds a position in a government or some other organization

omen event regarded as a sign of future happiness or disaster

prophecy message foretelling future events

record account, especially in writing, which keeps knowledge or information safe

ritual well-used form of a religious or traditional ceremony

sacrifice killing a person or animal as an offering to the gods

treachery betraying someone

tribute gifts given to a ruler by people

vengeful wanting to take revenge

Timeline

1299	Mexican people (Aztecs), travelling from lands to the north, reach Chapultepec near Lake Texcoco in Mexico
About 1325	Rise of the Aztecs in Mexico
About 1352	Acamapichtli is elected first king of the Aztecs
About 1436–1468	Rule of the Emperor Montezuma I of the Aztecs
About 1466	Birth of Montezuma II
About 1486–1502	Rule of the Aztec Emperor Ahuizotl
1492–93	Christopher Columbus reaches the Bahamas and West Indies
1499–1502	Amerigo Vespucci, a navigator from Florence, explores the coast of South America
1500	Aztec Empire reaches its biggest size under Emperor Ahuizotl
1502	Montezuma II becomes Emperor of the Aztecs after the death of his great-uncle Ahuizotl
1513	Juan Ponce de León, a Spanish explorer, becomes the first European to reach Florida
1517	The Spanish first reach the coast of Mexico
1519	Hernán Cortés and his Spanish soldiers reach Tenochtitlán
1520	Death of Montezuma
1521	Collapse of the Aztec Empire
1535	All of Aztec Empire ruled by Spain

Further reading & websites

Aztecs and Incas: a Guide to Two Great Empires in 1504, Sue Nicholson, Kingfisher, 2000

Aztecs: The Fall of the Aztec Capital, Richard Platt, Dorling Kindersley, 1999

Eyewitness Guides: Aztec, Elizabeth Baquedano, Dorling Kindersley, 1993

See Through History: The Aztecs, Tim Wood, Heinemann Library, 1992

Heinemann Explore – an on-line resource from Heinemann.
For Key Stage 2 history go to *www.heinemannexplore.com*

www.thehistorychannel.com

http://www.indians.org/welker/aztec.htm

All the Internet addresses (URLs) given in this book were valid at the time of going to press. However, due to the dynamic nature of the Internet, some addresses may have changed, or sites may have ceased to exist since publication. While the author and publishers regret any inconvenience this may cause readers, no responsibility for any such changes can be accepted by either the author or the publishers.